MARTHA JOE

Nulato

MARTHA JOE

Nulato

SPIRIT MOUNTAIN PRESS

ISBN: 0-910871-14-0

Interviewing and Editing:
Yvonne Yarber and Curt Madison

Photography:
Curt Madison (unless otherwise noted)

Material collected in Nulato March and September 1983 and November 1984.

Manuscript approved by Martha Joe November 1985.

**Library of Congress
Cataloging in Publication Data**

Madison, Curt
Yarber, Yvonne
Joe, Martha - Nulato. A Biography
YKSD Biography Series
ISBN 0-910871-14-0

1. Joe, Martha 2. Koyukon, Athabaskan
3. Alaska Biography

SPIRIT MOUNTAIN PRESS
P.O. BOX 1214 FAIRBANKS, ALASKA 99707

Produced and Funded by:
Yukon-Koyukuk School District of Alaska

Regional School Board:
Luke Titus - Chairman
Donald V. Honea - Vice Chairman
Neil Morris - Secretary
Patrick McCarty - Treasurer
Eddie Bergman
Cheryl DeHart
Patrick Madros

Superintendent: Joe Cooper
Assistant Superintendent: Fred Lau
Project Coordinator: Don Kratzer

Supplemental funding:
Johnson O'Malley Grant - EOOC14202516

Cover Photo:
Martha Joe with grandchildren in front of her lifelong home in Nulato, Thanksgiving Day, 1984.

Frontispiece:
Looking upriver towards the cemetery from the old village of Nulato, April 1983.

Acknowledgements

This book would not be possible without the help of many people. Martha Joe's daughter Mary Smith helped arrange interviews in Fairbanks. She and her sister Delores Kriska checked the family tree. Josephine Mountain conducted interviews in Koyukon with Martha Joe in Nulato. Eliza Jones encouraged expanded use of Koyukon because of Martha Joe's eloquence. She then did translations and provided typesetting of the Koyukon at Alaska Native Language Center of the University of Alaska. Liza Vernet again volunteered her keen eye for proofreading. Larry Laraby, Eva Bee, and Doug Miller do their stuff at Spirit Mountain Press. Joe Cooper, Fred Lau, and Mavis Brown persist through it all at Yukon-Koyukuk School District Central Office. And a special thanks to the Regional School Board who have been so patient supporting this project to its end.

This is the last book of the twenty part Yukon-Koyukuk Alaska Biography Series. Our sincere thanks to Bob Maguire whose original folly began this series nearly ten years ago. Our lives will never be the same. And finally, thanks to all the readers of the Series in Alaska and beyond who have made this work so rewarding.

Foreword

This book is the twentieth produced by the Yukon-Koyukuk School District in a series meant to provide cultural understanding of our own area and relevant role models for students. Too often Interior Alaska is ignored in books or mentioned only in conjunction with its mineral resources such as the gold rush or oil pipeline. We are gauged by what we are worth to Outside people. People living in the Interior certainly have been affected by those things but also by missionaries, wage labor, fur prices, celebrations, spring hunts, schools, technology, potlatches, and much more. For residents, Interior Alaska is all of those things people do together, whether in the woods, on the river, in the village or on Two Street. It's a rich and varied culture often glossed over in favor of things more easily written and understood.

This project was begun in 1977 by Bob Maguire. Representatives of Indian Education Parent Committees from each of Yukon-Koyukuk School District's eleven villages met in Fairbanks February of 1978 to choose two people from each village to write about. A variety of selection means were used—from school committees to village council elections. Despite the fact that most of the representatives were women, few women were chosen for the books. As the years passed, more women were added to give a more complete accounting of recent cultural changes.

It is our goal to provide a vehicle for people who live around us so they can describe the events of their lives in their own words. To be singled out as an individual as we have done in this series has not always been comfortable for the biographees, particularly for those who carry the strong Koyukon value of being humble. Talking about oneself has been a conflict overridden by the desire and overwhelming need to give young people some understanding of their own history in a form they have become accustomed to. A growing number of elders who can't read or write themselves think young people won't believe anything unless it's written in a book. This project attempts to give oral knowledge equal time in the schools.

As materials of this kind become more common, methods of gathering and presenting oral history get better. The most important ingredient is trust. After many hours of interview, people often relax to the point of saying some personal things they prefer left unpublished. After editing the tape transcripts we bring the rough draft manuscript back to the biographees to let them add or delete things before it becomes public. Too often those of us living in rural Alaska have been researched *on* or written *about* for an audience far away. This series is meant to bring information full round--from us back to us for our own uses.

Too many people in the Interior have felt ripped-off by journalists and bureaucrats. Hundreds pass through every year, all wanting information and many never to return. Occasionally their finished work may find its way back to the source only to flare emotions when people feel misrepresented. Perhaps a tight deadline or the lack of travel money may be the excuse for not returning for verification or approval. That is no consolation for people who opened up and shared something of themselves and are left feeling betrayed. We work closely with the biographees to check facts and intentions. The books need to be intimate and daring but the last thing we want to do is make someone's life more difficult. We need to share information in a wholesome way. After all, we're all in this together.

Comments about the biographies, their use, corrections, questions, or anything else is welcome.

Curt Madison
Yvonne Yarber
December 10, 1982
Manley Hot Springs
Alaska 99756

Table Of Contents

Introduction

Nulato has served as a meeting place for Athabaskan people since before dates were recorded. People would gather here from Kaiyuh Flats, Sislakaket, Unalakleet and the Koyukuk River. When the Russians tried to settle their North American colony, Nulato was as far as they got.

Malakov built a Russian trading post by the Nulato River in 1838. When he left for a few months, Natives burned it down. In 1839 he tried again with the same results. Three years later another Russian, Derabin, built a stronger fort at the present old village site. And in 1842 Lt. Zagoskin made his first expedition for Russia up the Yukon as far as Nulato. He explored the Koyukuk River and part of the upper Yukon during the next two years.

Competition for the riches of the fur trade grew more intense each year. The traditional route for manufactured items and tobacco began in Kotzebue and came by way of Koyukuk River Indians to the Interior. With the advent of the Russians in Nulato, a new route from Unalakleet by way of Kaiyuh Indians challenged the old one.

A series of raids between Koyukuk River and Kaiyuh Natives culminating in the 1851 battle known as the Nulato Massacre settled competition for trade. Koyukuk River supremacy, however, was not permanent. In 1854 a new fort was established that remained. Thirty years later sternwheeler steamboats brought gold-mad prospectors in a series of Alaska rushes. Nulato became a main stop for supplies, and the site of the first Catholic mission.

Nulato is the upriver home of the Stickdance, a sacred Athabaskan memorial to the recent dead. Held every couple years, it is an important spiritual event of the Interior.

Martha Joe is everyone's grandmother — partly from the respect she has earned during her 90 years, and partly from the many children she raised. She carries within her the history of the Kaiyuh people. She was raised in the old ways learning the skills of fur sewing and mid-wifery. She had some mission schooling and an early forced marriage. She is the most eloquent of Koyukon speakers yet living. And she owns a radio that gets Chinese broadcasts.

This book could not contain all her stories. Those people lucky enough to know Martha Joe have heard many more.

A home in Nulato, April 1983.

Nulato taken from the graveyard hill 1982.

"This is Nulato when it was just getting started. I remember that house closest to the bank about half-way down. The big building in front was Leo Demoski's house. After they moved away Dalquists got it. It is still here today."

"They bring all that wood in for the steamboats. Mostly they cut it from back on the Nulato River in the winter and haul it in. But some of it they get in the summer and drift it down from upriver. About all the steamboats burned wood. That's why there were so many people staying around here. The large building is the hospital built in 1908." Note the birchbark canoe on the beach and the fish wheel off the point. Circa 1910."

Local Area

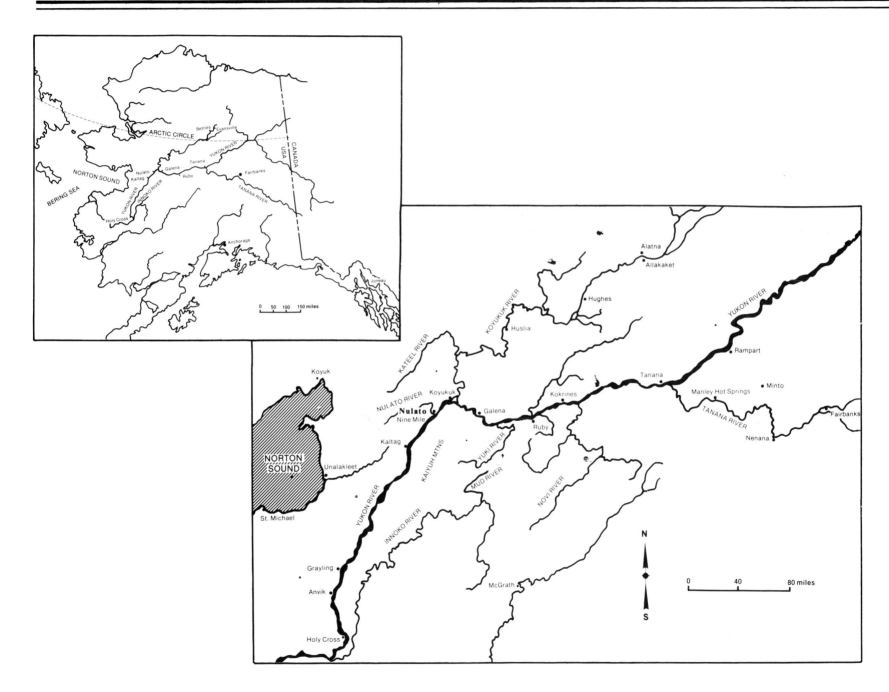

Chapter One: The Way I Heard It

Noolaaghadoh

This village used to be down by the Nulato River, where they called *Noolaaghadoh*. That means the main place to catch dog salmon in the summertime. That's why they called it *Noolaaghadoh*. This place, where my house is, they called *Tlaakiyeet* on account of the big bluff there.

There were no moose around here. People had to go over to the Innoko River to hunt. They go over the hills. It would take about a month to get one or two moose. Then they haul it in. Two or three or four families go in a bunch. Those that are able to go, go with their husbands. If they got too many kids, they have to stay.

In my young days it was a hard time. Old people mostly took care of themselves. Those old grandpas I've seen with their wives, as much as they were able, they took care of themselves. Even some of them all bent over. Still they traveled in boats.

They travel to where they could make their living. Springtime and falltime they go to Kaiyuh. Lots of

Oregon Province Jesuit Archives

"This is my first husband's parents Mareena and Gregory Esmailka. My first in-laws half-breed Russian. Altogether I saw five half-breed Russians. Antoski, Karrilka, Kriska, Esmailka, and Demoski." Circa 1910.

people went out. Some of them die in Kaiyuh and they bring the bodies in. I used to see it when I was a little kid. Sometimes they bury them where they die. In Kaiyuh there's lots of graves here and there. That's where our people come from.

The Russians had a place right here first, the way I heard it when I was a little girl. Kozevnikoff whose grandson is in Tanana was here with a store. And other people had stores here, I guess. I didn't understand that very well. People moved here for those stores a little at a time, downriver people and Kaiyuh people. That's how it became big right here.

Down at the old village is where the warriors fought and killed people. I never saw it, but I heard about it. I've seen the place. It's hump-like, full of grass where they had all the houses. After the battle people never go back there. I heard a lot of people talk about it and I saw the man who escaped.

"Two stores in this picture. There used to be lots of stores. They changed every year." Nulato about 1910.

The One Who Escaped

This account of the February 16th, 1851, battle commonly called the Nulato Massacre is paraphrased from an interview done in Koyukon by Josephine Mountain with Martha Joe. The translation was done by Eliza Jones of the Alaska Native Language Center. A complete transcription in Koyukon immediately follows this story.

I'm now going to talk about the man who escaped the war at Nulato in 1851. His name was *Diloghahudaatłggunh*, and I saw him. I think he died in 1906. He was an old man when I saw him. He was sitting there, old and blind and bald-headed. People were sitting around listening. Tears were coming down his face as he talked.

He was visiting from up the Kaiyuh to this place where a potlatch was taking place. It is said he was somehow related to a medicine man who loaned him his ground squirrel parka. This parka would help him escape from trouble.

"You know the place that you're going to, I can see trouble there. I want you to wear my ground squirrel parka," this medicine man told *Diloghahudaatłggunh*. That is what he did.

There were a lot of people at that place, people from the coast, Unalakleet, downriver and *Kkaayah* (Kaiyuh) area. During the night after everybody had gone to bed, it is said that all of a sudden they started hearing noises outside. Then the man whose house *Diloghahudaatłggunh* was staying at said, "What is all that noise outdoors at night? Why are people walking around?" They say it was Minook's grandfather who said this. He was a young man then and living there with his family.

Minook's grandfather got up from across the room and said, "How unusual! Why are people walking around at night? Usually people only walk around during the day." Saying this, he walked out the door. All of a sudden they heard him scream out! He barely staggered back into the house. His poor wife cried out, "Somebody has hurt my husband!"

Then someone in the house said, "Even so, let's all try to be quiet. Let's all be quiet. I think a war party has come." They weren't staying in a regular winter house because of the shortage of houses. There were so many people visiting some were forced to stay in the summer houses that had posts for the walls.

And this man who escaped the war quickly crawled back to the wall and began pulling some of the poles up that made the wall. He kept pulling on them until he loosened some of them. Then he squeezed out between the loosened poles and quickly went back to the cache. He felt around the edge of the cache and came upon a pair of snowshoes. One side was a woman's snowshoe and the other a man's. Right away he attached them to his feet. While the warriors were busy blocking the exits and smokeholes of the houses with boards he took off towards the portage trail.

He kept going without stopping until he rushed out to this lake. He was traveling as fast as he could when all of a sudden he saw people standing in a row in the middle of the lake. He thought to himself, "Well I'm already here, no use stopping now, either way I'm dead." He just kept on going. Meanwhile he got his hunting knife ready. "I don't know what I could do with a hunting knife against bows and arrows but that was all I had," he said.

He just kept on going towards this line of people in the lake. He soon realized that the warriors had taken off their parkas and put them on sticks to look like people. It was only parkas to scare off anybody who might have escaped.

From there he said he took off down towards that little river that comes out down there, the Nulato River. "I crossed over to the other side of the river. There I took a rest and caught my breath." He said he wasn't even himself he got so scared when he had seen some of the people being killed.

"I was there catching my wind when all of a sudden I saw a mother and child come out across there. Apparently then had snuck out the same wall I had gone through." The one who was to become Minook's grandfather, was a little boy then. It was him and his mother.

To his dismay he suddenly saw a war party come out behind them. He said he took off again. The war party came up behind and shot an arrow at them. The little boy was shot but it only grazed his skin. He threw himself in the snow. Apparently his mother told him, "If you are wounded but not hurt bad, just throw yourself into the snow as though you were dead." That is what he did. She was shot with an arrow in the breast and threw herself in the snow also. They laid there a long, long time.

They got up again when they felt certain there was no one around. They waited till they could not hear any noise before they began following *Diloghahɥdaatɭggunh*'s tracks. They crawled because they had no snowshoes. Finally they came out to the Yukon at Two Mile and headed downriver where there were lots of camps.

Diloghahɥdaatɭggunh headed across the Yukon back toward *Kkaayah*, back to Kaiyuh. By then he said it was just like daylight from the houses they were burning down. It was just bright. "So then, when I crossed the Yukon, I crawled up the riverbank and there I sat down. I broke some standing willows and I sat on that. It was raining below my eyes. There were just tears running down when I saw what was happening over there. Meanwhile I saw two people following my tracks coming across the Yukon. They had followed me. They were walking out on the river among the rough ice. It looked like they were going to come ashore but they kept stopping here and there. They kept looking towards the shore."

Then they turned around and started back. "I had thought that if they were going to come up the bank, I was going to club them over the head just as their heads appeared over the bank. But they turned around first."

This was part of the war party. They had followed him because someone had seen him escape. Meanwhile the mother and child had gone downriver. There used to be lots of camps down that way so they let the people know that there was a war party on the way.

So then he took off towards the Kaiyuh and let everybody up that way know what had happened. Everyone armed themselves and were prepared but the war party didn't go any farther.

My old grandma, my dad's grandmother, was also saved from the massacre as a little girl. The head of the war party had apparently said "Save this little girl who is named after my wife. Her name is *Nokkaak'ideelno.*" This is what the person said who started the war. And when they saved this girl,

Curt Madison

Yvonne Yarber tape recording Martha Joe while she tells the story of "The One Who Escaped" in Koyukon. Josephine Mountain (left) was the translator during the interview. November 1982.

she was wearing a belt that was made in the image of rosehips out of trade beads. When a man saw this belt on her he walked over to her and said, "Oh what a pretty thing my grandchild is wearing. What a pretty belt she's wearing."

He went over to her to untie this belt and take it away. This person named *Hayolol* walked over to him and pushed his face away with a bow and said to him, "That is not your stuff. Is that what you saved her life for? You leave her alone." And pushed him away with his bow.

That is how we are here today, from this grandmother who was saved from the war. This was my daddy's grandmother who was saved because of a name, *Nokkaak'ideelno*. Without that name she would have gone with everybody else. It is said that she didn't want to be saved.

This is a real sad story and it was the Koyukuk River people who had done this. I don't know why. That's the one thing I didn't find out. People used to talk about it but I don't know the reasons. That's a real sad story. They used to cry when they talk about it. It was real sad. They said they heard a lot of women holler while they burned up in the fire.

This is the story I used to hear when I was a little girl but I didn't pay much attention then. I heard the person telling the story but I didn't pay much attention. Then I heard the story again later from my dad who had heard it directly from *Diloghahʉdaatɫggunh*.

Nimaah Donoghadiyoninh

Ts'a eey dodo eey nimaah donoghadiyoninh koonh. Naaghtɫ-'aan'. Diloghahʉdaatɫggunh meezneeninh eesee naghtɫ-'aaninh. 1906 hʉt'aanh didiyoh. He was old ts'a ant'aa eey naaghtɫ-'aan'.

Nodaggu Kkaayah hʉts'inh gheelhee yooduhts'a na'aho, go neehootaaɫt'onh ts'idnee dinh. Eet gheel haɫda milots'aa eeydinh haɫda dik'ahʉndaggaz da'aak yʉgh neeneeɫkooɫ meeznee. "'Tɫ'eegho ts'eedaah dahoot'aa eendinh hʉts'a taaleeyo, da nʉgh sik'ahʉndaggaz da'aak nidaanlikooɫ, yiɫnee," meeznee. Ʉhts'a haɫda didiyoh.

Ts'ʉhʉ go tɫ'eegho dinaa hooleenh. Nonɫits'a hʉyiɫ hadnee. Nodo' hʉtsinh hʉyiɫ, nodaggu Kkaayah hʉts'inh hʉyiɫ.

Eet gheelhee yoogh naaɫidzit gheelhee. Hooɫ soot'a gheelhee haadok'idiniyh. Do'oogha hʉts'a kk'ots'eedidaaɫ. Ahʉyiɫ, "hee ginee tɫidaaɫ dohʉdnee? Ts'a do'oogh kk'ots'eedidaaɫ?" nee gheelhee go yʉgh yah lidoninh. Haɫda Minook mito' eeydinh mito' keel yoz nilaanh ts'a gheelhee donts'inh haɫda hadaadlitɫ'ee. Eet yah gheel hadoneeyohee. "Hʉyiɫ yoonots'a hʉndinh nin' okko taatɫneek," yiɫnee eey go this

20

man. "Dzigee! Dohʉt'aanh ts'a go kk'otłee'eelteeyh? Dzaanh ta hʉyaan' eesee kk'ots'eedidaał," nee ts'a tłeetaalyo. Ahuyił hʉndinh k'idoditaadlaghał eetł'akk gheelhee. Doo'! Nonts'a hadononaal'ot. Hʉyił hʉndinh, "'Go sakkun' ts'ilaatłghaanh,' ditaalnee'," meeznee go sołt'aanh yok'aala. "Eenhda hʉyił tłaa dodaalʉhlilik. Ogee yʉhts'a hʉyił asiniyh," nee. "Nimaah ditaalnee' ts'a hʉyił asiniyh," nee.

Yʉhʉts'a naahʉloo yah dahooleel. Ogee yoogh saanh yah tʉh gheel eey daats'a dinhoogheet'aa'ee, poles aahaa. Eet gheel hʉts'a hamaanhʉdaadlaggaat eey neełts'a nidididaahna. Yʉhʉts'a da'eet'aal ts'a yʉhʉts'a nonggʉt neetłooggadaaldaatł. Ts'iyʉhts'a doogh yʉhts'a konhyeets'a yʉhts'a dikinh yił niditagheeniyh. Dikinh hʉʉndaatłkkat. Eet daa'an yʉhʉts'a tłee'eeditsuł. Ts'ʉhʉz nonggʉ yʉhz da'eet'aa'aa ts'iyʉhʉts'a . . . Soot'a notłoogh yah hʉghonheełneeyh gheelhee. Hʉdont'aakk'ʉł-haditolaał hu hʉdonk'ahadiłtuts, k'aazaalzaaga'.

Ts'ʉhʉz nonggʉ dʉhdził ghʉ neeneeyo. Ts'ʉh doogh dʉhdził doogh kk'aamaan nidilniyh. Hooł oyh milotł'ʉgh gheedaatł meeznee. Sołt'aanh oya' go k'eełakk'ee, go k'eełakk'ee hałda dinaayoo oya'.

Ts'ʉhʉts'a adeehu yʉh sakkaa' anlitłluyh. Ts'ʉhʉts'a naangga teek'otłeeneetonh hu dʉhʉsloh. Naa' lisdleedaa neets'in'," nee.

"Ahʉyił hʉndinh nonggʉ meenkk'a hadineeghasakkʉyhtł. Hʉyił yoonługh hʉnda koon nozaalyo. 'Adeehu yidon koon silaadlaghaanh', yeenisdlinh. Ts'ʉh nonła yʉhʉ . . . Digo tł'akk'aadee'on hałda oolsneek," nee. "Eenhda maahaa dotaaghsneel soo'oo? Kk'o yideet'eeyhna dint'aa daa' soo'u? Ts'iyʉh nonła yʉh . . . At'eeyło yʉhʉts'a hadida'aaga ło yʉhts'a anonk'ahanaatłghał łonh," nee. Hałda k'idonotodolinh okko. Eet nodo' ts'iyʉhʉz dʉhʉsloh," nee. Ts'ʉh eey no'o sahna dotlin ło dahooloh, hodee nodo little slough ts'aahʉdaanee'o hu. "Nodo' nonots'a sahna dots'in nononsiyo. Eet nosiyhligitseenh," nee.

Eey go yʉh adideenh, dzaadolghał ts'in'. Go bʉnghʉł dinaasaalghonh. "Ts'a yoogh eet yʉh tł'odaalsido. Huyił nonots'a hʉnda koon neełonhyoo ts'aanee'ots. At'eeyło eey go sakk'a yʉh tłeeheeditsuł łonh," nee.

Eey go Minook mitseek'aal tolaalinh little boy, eey go maanh yił. X! [gasp] Gin yagga hamakk'a ts'aahʉnaadiyoot gheelhee. Eet eey go ts'iyʉhts'a koon tł'enołiyo. Ts'iyʉhts'a hamak'a ts'aahʉnaadiyoot. Ts'a gheelhee hʉhooneek'inh. Huyił go keel yoz miłt'i łik'inh. Ts'ʉh kitł yee hok'idolghał. At'eeyło maanh diyłnee ts'in'. "Yagga yoogh nʉgh siyh hʉtaałineek kk'a da'eent'aa daa' hok'ideenghoolghaas," yiłnee łonh. "Go adinh hałda go mit'uga łik'inh. Ts'ʉh odeekoon kił yee hok'idinolghaats. Ts'ʉhʉts'a gin yagga eet hagheetaa', hagheetaa'. Ts'ʉhʉts'a kk'ʉdaa soot'a haanodok'ahadeeniyhdlaa kk'aant'aa ts'ʉhʉz gheel kk'ʉdaa eey go dinaa neeyo hu yʉhʉ tłooggahadolyaał, oyh adeenh. Ts'ʉhʉts'a eey go Yookkana, eey nʉgh Two Mile donʉhts'inh, Yookkan hałdee' hokk'aa haghee'ots. Tsʉhʉ nodo' dʉhʉhooloh. Well! Lots of camps hʉdeegheelaa', ahu hałda hadok'ahʉhdagheełneek. Dahoono adinh hałda nonaan Kkayah hʉts'a dinohooloh.

"Go hak'eeldzaayh," nee. "Go kk'ʉdaa hʉyee ditaałakk'onh ts'ʉhʉts'a hałda hak'eeldzaayh," nee. "Ts'a nʉgh tł'odoggʉ honolsiyo da hałda kk'ʉdaa dotł'odinaalsido," nee. "Eey go kkun' nitł-'aanh da hałda singh yagga ałkonh. Dahoono donłits'a hałda sakk'a noho'ʉstł," hʉlnee. "Eey go sakk'a hʉkk'a daahal'ots ts'in'," hʉlnee. "Eenda neenaahataałt'is, neenaahataałt'is. Nonłits'a hałda hʉhʉneeł'aanh. Hooł yagga k'its'a naahadaal'ots," hʉlnee. "'Well! Go yʉhts'a eey go yʉhʉ tł'odoggʉ hotłaahotłiyhtł da yʉhʉ, go daayagga tł'eeyagga yʉhʉts'a hamitłeeyeek'itaaghst'ahtł,' hamoodeeghsnee'," nee.

Ts'a yʉhʉts'a gheel eey haano'eediyo. Ts'ʉhʉts'a hadok'ʉhʉdagheełneek. Eet gheel nahootaadliyonh. Eenda gheel nodot hʉts'inh k'its'a naahadaaldaatł hʉhʉdnee.

Eet gheel hałda sitsook'aal, eey go eetaa mitsook'aala eeydinh hałda k'idaaghaltaanh ts'idnee.

"Yagga sa'ot ano'oolzeeninh Nokkaak'ideelno k'ido'oohłtaał," nee ts'a gheel hʉgh needok'idaanee'onh eey go nimaah k'idoyona'. Eey go magha'an noyeeyh ditaalnee'anh. Gin ghʉ soo'?

"Eeydinh gheel hałda kooyh yeega' yoonaan yoo'an hʉk'inildila' aahaa gheel haliłdlikił. Eeydee gheelhee, go dinaa mʉgh neeneeyo. 'Geen zoo' go sikoy yoza yaahaa haliłdlikilee', yiłnee dahoono gheel dakk'ayitaal'ʉh. Ahuyił Hayołoł gheel yʉgh neeneeyo. Tł'eełtin' aahaa dagga yaanaaneelit. Dahoono, 'Mideeloy yił anaa' midilʉhnee' ts'a ło maahaa taahoolʉh'oy haanh. Mik'oda eeydinh,' yiłnee dahoono dagga yaak'ineelit, eey go ditł'eełtin aahaa," hayłnee.

Uhts'a hoghoda gheel go dinaahoolaanee. Tsook'aal yon k'idaaghaltaanh eey go Eetaa mitsook'aala Nokkaak'ideelno, oos gha'an k'idaaghaltaanee.

The rest of this book is written from interviews with Martha Joe in English.

Cold

It was real cold in the old days. Colder than it is now. We had reindeer parkies and rabbit skins. Then we had overparkies, too. Those were made out of heavy canvas or cotton drill. I used to make rabbit skin rope and cover it with calico or thin blankets to keep the hair from falling off. It's warm. And rabbit skin mitts and socks. That way they don't feel the cold no matter how cold it is. People were crazy to buy those thin blanket sheets of flannel. Such nice colors and striped on the end. They go after it for lining the rabbit skin blanket. But nowadays I don't see it no more. Maybe it's because us old people are going away and nobody buys it much.

I don't know how cold it was long time ago. They didn't have thermometers, but they find out by the trees. When the trees get snowy frosty, it's cold. It means the trees are dressed warm. When it's frosty white like that they don't go out. Some people used to freeze to death, too. One old man froze between here and Kaltag coming back from visiting Unalakleet. People coming up with teams found him. Maybe he was walking to one of the camps, but he froze before he reached there.

"This is my daddy Peter Antoski. They started calling him Peter Chief because he was the first elected chief of Nulato. He helped with hunting for the potlatches and stuff but he only stayed chief for two or three years." Circa 1910.

Medicine People

I've seen all different kinds of medicine people, but the strongest ones died before I remember. They used to say my grandfather, my auntie's father, was a strong one. I don't know his name. He had a son from one of his wives. In those days they used to have two wives. That son became a medicine man after his dad. He's the one they say discovered wine.

He had a big new tent. People were all around inside the tent. Then he started to spin around, the way they get when they make medicine. He told them to hang a pan way up at the end of the tent. While he was spinning around the people heard something hollering in the pan. When they took the pan down it was full of something like tea. He told them to pass it around. They say it tasted good just like whiskey.

Lots of people seen that time, even my daddy. Father MacElmeel came out to find out for sure what happened. Those days they used to sit out in front by the river on warm spring days. One Sunday he came and started to ask questions of people. He asked who drank some. Those that did told him, "Me."

Medicine people finally just went away. They die off with sickness or sometimes it's a sudden death. They get sick just like other people.

"This is my stepmother Gooleek. Her name is Ellen and Gooleek. She had light colored eyes and curly hair. Half-breed. My momma died in 1914 on Christmas day trying to give birth to Arthur. It was on account of my little brothers that my daddy married her in 1917. I raised Arthur because even though I was married we didn't have any kids yet of our own. My daddy told me to raise kids. 'Cause if you get old, you will be helpless. Even if you get a cup of water, it will be hard for you to get it,' he told me. That's how come I raised kids."

Chapter Two: Wake Up To Life

Born At Camp

I was born way downriver at camp. My folks used to stay there. My grandparents and great-grandparents, too. Sixty miles below Kaltag, *K'aghasdokkaakk'at*, on an island on the north bank of the Yukon River. They call it Doom Creek now. Kaltag people know it well. September 6, 1896, they say I was born. I don't know, maybe. My mommy and daddy said it was while the slush was starting to run on the river. Maybe October. I'm eighty-six years old already now (1982).

Those days midwives carry the woman that's going to have the baby. They put them in their laps. They say my mom had a hard time with me. At the day's end, at midnight, I was born.

My daddy's name used to be Peter, Peter Antoski. That's the one that raised me. They didn't use last names usually. Antoski is the one that raised him. My mom's name was Elizabeth. They both had Indian names, too. Mom was *Maats'ineelno* and dad was *Neelkk'aayineekaalt'onh*.

They raised me pretty strict. They wouldn't let me go out or play with the other kids. They wouldn't let me have friends. In Indian they call it temptation.

When I first wake up to life I remember my mother was cleaning me up, combing my hair. She said something about school, but I don't know what school means. That was 1902. She was cleaning me up to take me to the sister's mission school.

We didn't have books like they do nowadays. Most of the people, womens and grandpas, didn't talk English. Just the sisters, priests, and storekeepers spoke English. And we didn't keep going steady to school in those days. We had to go out to camp in the fall and spring. We're out until the first part of

December and back out again in April. After breakup, not long after Easter Sunday, we come back from Kaiyuh in a row boat. My daddy built the boat and my brother Aloysius rowed. Yukon boats they called them. They didn't last for a long time.

In school we had big charts hanging on the wall. The first words I learned were c-a-t cat and r-a-t rat. Sometimes it was just like a dream. I start to pick it up a little but we had our Indian prayer books, too, and we didn't learn much English. We didn't go at English words much because we used the Indian prayer books that Father Jetté wrote.

The sisters would ask us what is this word and we know it already. They would write Indian words to church songs on the board. The sisters get it from Father Jette's books. That way we didn't learn much English. And then we used to go out in September to our camps. Stay there all fall till the first part of December. That's the only way we used to like to live. And not much White

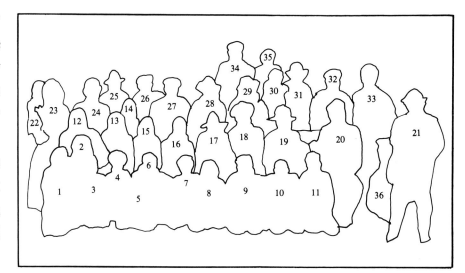

Martha Joe Collection

Group of Kaltag people see inset for identification: 1-11 unidentified; 12. Marie Nikolai; 13. Twenty-two Mile Mary; 14. unidentified; 15. Agatha Silas Andre; 16. Pauline Pitka; 17. Nick; 18. George Semaken; 19. Jack Nikolai; 20. Paul; 21. Adolph Miller; 22. unidentified baby; 23. Mrs. Tin Can Chief; 24. Alexie; 25. Smokey Joe; 26. Hooligan; 27. Nick Nikolai; 28. John Sirosky; 29. John Nikolai; 30. unidentified baby; 31. Jack Kaltag; 32. Big Jim; 33-35. unidentified.

26

people. Only White people I saw were the priest, the sisters, and the storekeeper.

When I was small my folks start to travel with me. They left that place downriver in 1898 and went to Circle City. My dad was a deckhand on the steamboat so we all traveled together. Lots of Native people were pilots because the captains didn't know the river and they showed them.

In Circle City it was gold rush days. They had saloons and roadhouses like my folks never saw before. They didn't talk about it much but that's how I know because I was still a baby. I didn't wake up to it. My brother Aloysius was born at Eagle.

They were doing labor work, but they didn't stay long. The next year they came down to here. They built a cabin somewhere in the village, but I don't know exactly where. They're supposed to belong to downriver but they wanted to stay here. That must have been in 1899. They were related to people from way below Kaltag, but they all died off now. Daddy was from Kaiyuh and Mom was from way downriver where I was born. Before they got married she was at Holy Cross Mission for about a year.

The sisters wanted to send me to Holy Cross, too. But my daddy didn't want it. He said his sister died there and maybe he thought I was going to die there, too. After they built a cabin here we only

Martha Peters Joe, Nulato. Circa 1913.

"That's Irene Demoski on the left and my sister Lucy Peters at Holy Cross. Irene married Minook so they called her Irene Minook and my sister married Joe Stickman. She was younger than me. I was born in 1896 and she was born in 1902. That's why I don't have any memory now. I'm pretty old and I don't care much now. I just gave up." Circa 1914.

stayed here and out at Kaiyuh. We spent fall and spring out there. Just the middle of the winter we stayed in Nulato.

No matter how swift the water was we had to row the boat. No engine those days for us. Sometimes we got tired. We were a little too weak those days. It used to take two nights to get to camp. Daddy went ahead in a canoe until he got something to eat for the night. Then he came back and helped us row. Our mom used a paddle to steer while we were rowing. The dogs followed us on the land.

We all took all the groceries we needed for the fall in the boat with us. But in Kaiyuh we had lots of things to eat like ducks and good fish. When we get to Kaiyuh the women put in fishnets and catch lots of fish. Men spend two days getting ducks. There was no moose and no beaver. Just ducks and bears and porcupines. We enjoyed the food, because it was nice.

Sometimes our grub doesn't last with us and we have to rush down to the store and get more grub after it freezes up. In the spring-time we have enough because there's lots to eat off the country. No problem in the spring, but in the fall we get out of grub because it's a long time. Three months we're out and not enough boats to carry what we need. We get along. People get along.

"The boy on the left is my brother Aloysius Peters. He is the one who died in 1981. My father made those snowshoes. Next is Fred Stickman, Margaret Kriska, Julia Kriska; and Wilson. This must have been taken around 1912."

Steamboat loading at Nulato circa 1910.

Usually we just bring the main things we need like sugar, flour, lard, coffee, tea and rice. And dry fruit if we can get it in wooden boxes. We cook dried apples and rice separate then eat them together. We have to eat whatever our mother serve us. We don't know. We eat what they serve and later on we find out how to eat it.

After the men get through putting in a fishtrap, they go up in the hills after bears. They stay out for a couple days until they get luck. Sometimes they kill one bear and are satisfied with it. They have something to bring home. Sometimes they get two bears. They cut all the meat off the bones and carry it on their backs. They have to go a long ways up into the hills to where the bears are eating berries.

After that they tend to the fishtraps and put up a lot of pike and white fish. There are some places you can catch loche, too. Fat fish, oh! They're nice.

The ducks we either put in salt in a barrel or split and hang in the smokehouse for awhile. That way they don't get rotten. Bear meat, too, they smoke a little bit and hang in the cache with the ducks. We have to save that for our food and for potlatch supply. Nowadays with freezers it's a lot easier.

A lot of people used to be in camp. Now it is just quiet. We used to hear dogs hollering and shooting from here and there. Must have been five or six villages in different places in Kaiyuh.

Old Man Silas and Esmailka lived the closest to us. We used to feed their dogs for them. The kids used to come to play hockey in the slough. It was lots of fun. We looked for bent sticks and carved them down. Then we made a ball out of birch. The balls were strong. They never cracked. Lot of times I got hit by a stick and fell down. Sometimes I had a hard time walking for a couple days. But I got right back in there. That was our fun.

"Mrs. Stickman and Mrs. Silas. We used to visit Mrs. Silas in Kaiyuh because they lived nearby us. The boy is Walter Stickman, the youngest one. He was crippled."

We used to have Stickdance every winter. All the people that spread out around here and up the Koyukuk River come together. When we start we get up about three o'clock, start to move around. About five or six we hook up and start out. Everybody gathers at Dinnertime Camp. There's one place we all stop. Gee, it's nice to see people coming down. Sometimes ten teams strung out on the trail.

In 1908 there was a gold rush to Iditarod. The miners put in a short cut trail over the hills from here. Short cut but it still takes five hours to go with a good team. We used to have nine or eleven dogs in our team. I would ride in the sled with the bedding and all the kids while my husband rode on the runners.

We used to take care of our dogs just like they were human beings. When you've got good dogs you can travel any place. The most kids I had was five at one time. All of us in the sled was a big load, but our dogs never gave up till the end of the day when it's time to stop. That's the kind of dogs we had. Nowadays only racers take care of dogs.

I was up there this spring. I want to be out so they take me out every spring. Harold put up a lumber house for me and I stay there with my daughter Lawana Sommers. It was quiet. No dogs hollering, no sounds. Just my daughter and I went to Kaiyuh. Used to be lots of people, but they're all gone now.

Since this school got started in Nulato, nobody goes out any more. People don't know how to hunt the old-timer way. They don't know how to make sleds, snowshoes, fishtraps, and things like that. Only some smart guys know how to make sleds.

All the people that did those things died away. Me and that grandma back there, Martha Brush, are the oldest ones now. Two of us, that's all. All the young kids here don't know how to talk our Native language. Nowadays the language is nothing to them. It's all the White people side. Easy living.

Doctor and Priests

In 1908 and 1909 I stayed with Dr. Norton and his wife to babysit. I lived the whole winter with them. When we came in from camp in the fall they picked me up. I don't know how they find me. Well, I been with the sisters a couple times. Maybe that way they find out I know how to say yes and no, talk a little bit English.

In the spring they got on the boat to go Outside. That's the time they want me to go out with them, but my daddy didn't want me to go. I don't know why. They said they'd take me out, put me through school to learn to be a teacher. But my daddy was pretty strict to send me away. That's why I didn't go.

When I stayed with the doctor we lived at the hospital at the end of town. I used to visit my parents only on Sunday. My mamma used to bring me up there at six o'clock Sunday evening. Once a week I visit my parents. Them olden days it was strict with us girls. Not like nowadays.

"This is one Sunday in 1908 and we're going out for a reindeer ride. On the left is Dr. Albert Norton holding his baby Francis Kemp and his wife Eva Bertha Soul Norton in front. Next to her is my uncle Ted Ketlaanee. The government had a big reindeer herd about two miles from here and he was hired to be the herder. My uncle Joseph nicknamed Onion is holding the rope and next to him is the carpenter who built the house. He was bent over from a hunchback. His name was something like Poisnaker, I don't know how to spell it. I was inside getting dressed. That's why I'm not in the picture."

I wouldn't go out at night and I wouldn't even have friends. They used to say I'd go wild. And them days it was not as bad as right now. Fred Clark, Snow, and Dan Avery was all that had a saloon and roadhouse. They had one Filipino man was a cook for them named Harry Lapin. That was the first time I saw a Filipino.

I didn't see much drink. The Indians were quarantined from liquor that time and White people start to get it for them. I know my daddy used to feel good sometimes but I didn't see him get very drunk like people nowadays. He always used to keep a bottle in the trunk for us for medicine. He used to call it brandy and it had a hole in the bottom. When we get a cold or sick they used to put some in hot water for us and put us to bed. That way we get healed up right away. The cold would go away from us the next day.

N.C. Co. store in Nulato about 1910.

"Malya Esmailka. She was married to Tommy Esmailka, my husband's oldest brother. She used to talk English pretty good because she spent three years at Holy Cross." Circa 1912.

Maybe he learned that in Circle City.

The priests and sisters were pretty strict. I used to listen to them, of course, I was with these White people and they were strong Catholics, too. Then the couple running the N.C. Store were strong Catholics. I worked for them after I got married. They knew I was with White people before. And I didn't know much what was going on because I didn't go running around. That's the way things were. And then a good many of the people been to Holy Cross. I didn't go, me. Maybe I'd do better if I went to Holy Cross, but my daddy don't want me to go.

I don't know much about the early missionaries because I didn't wake up to it until they took me to school in 1902. Since that time I start to know things little at a time.

Some of them talk in Native. I know Father Rossi talked pretty good and understand it. He was strict with people, but Father Jetté was the expert one. He used to be interpreter for those that go to jails. He would go to Fairbanks and be interpreter for them. That was a good Father. I don't see how he learned, maybe from the boys at the mission. He made books, too, in Indian. Somebody took my copy. I had two but I gave one to Madeline. She asked me for it and I didn't want to turn her down because she is my friend. Father Loyens gave me one too, but the kids destroyed it. I miss it.

All Indian language in that book. Just prayers and songs but it's our language and I understand it real good. It's way different from the way our language used to be because it's up the river language, but I understand it. I can sing it but I got no voice now. I'm too old.

People all miss Father Rossi because he used to talk in Native and pray in Native. He used to travel around to the camps alone in the summertime. Pulling his boat along with a rope upstream. He used to go to Kaltag alone. And no kicker them days. Poor Father. Nice priest they even talk about him yet. When they see this priest flying around they say, "Where is poor old Father Rossi, used to drive dogs, and pull around?"

Oregon Province Jesuit Archives

"Father Rossi, he's the one that preached in Indian and taught us songs. He was a favorite father." Photo circa 1910.

When a Girl Becomes a Woman

It's a long story about how a girl becomes a woman. I can tell you but I don't think young people now would believe it. Things are very different nowadays.

We were told we would step on a needle. They don't tell us straight out. But it's their way, the old fashioned way. And they tell us to watch ourself when we run around. Don't run around too much, you might run on the needle. And that's when I became a woman. I was running around with

33

kids, playing outdoors.

Right away I ran home and sneaked under the bed. Just like I knew what happened. I knew what it means. When we become women we don't stay outdoors in front of everybody. We're not even supposed to be seen after that. So I stayed under the bed while my mom was out cutting fish.

She came in and hollered for me, "Where are you? Go down and hang fish," she told me. But I stayed there. She hollered and hollered for me. Finally I answered her. I said, "Hey." That's all.

That's all the answer I gave her, but she guessed. She went out for my daddy. She told my daddy in secret that a little room had to be fixed up for me. Where I'm going to stay. They got white canvas drill cloth and put it around the corner of their bed. I have to get out and wait on top of the bed. Nobody would come in, other kids, even my brothers and sisters.

So they put me in there with my little bedding, a reindeer skin for a mattress and one blanket. I had my pillow and my certain things. And I start to stay there. For two nights they never gave me nothing, not even a swallow of water. Well, I have to take it. I have to do what I'm told. Hard, those days.

Then the morning after two days, my daddy brought in two old women to talk to me about

"Ba'oozkkalhaanh, *her name means no name in English. Even when she was old, she was pretty.*" *Circa 1912.*

34

the experience of my life. They gave me an explaining about what I should be, what I should do for the home. One told me that she had things, always had things, something to eat in the cache. Some nice things to eat that she worked for in the summer. The other one told me that she had been sewing. She was a good sewer. She could make parkies and all that. I took that. I understood them. We got to just take it the way we're told.

After that they gave a cupful of rotten grease. My! I couldn't take it but I have to take it. I just gobble it down. When a girl throws up the grease it means she will have a short life. I didn't throw up. I wanted to vomit, but I don't know why I didn't. Then they gave me water and after that they fed me.

The reason they gave the grease is so I wouldn't eat much. This was important especially when there's hard times and not much food. A little food would sustain me for a long time. Also, if I eat too much it would take my husband's luck away. Just like I'll eat up his luck. That's the reason for drinking the grease.

They told me not to sleep too much. If I sleep too much, I'll be lazy. So they gave me a willow stick and told me to sit on my bedding. When I was feeling sleepy I put my head on my hands propped up on that stick. When I fell asleep the stick would fall and I would wake up. That way I wouldn't sleep much. I never laid down to sleep. I just sit up with that stick till I couldn't do it anymore that night. Then I go to bed. Every night we do that for about a month. I never sleep much after that. Even now.

I was in that place for three months. It was just as big as a bed. I never get up. Never go out even to the outhouse. They just bring me can and empty it out like in the hospital. Just stay in that little place. My! They used to do that for the woman's beauty and light complexion. I've seen lots of old women, long time ago, that have been that way. Their bodies get white, like half-breeds, and they have black hair. They're bright. Me, I've got white hair.

Sitting down for that long my legs got weak. I could hardly walk. They told me to walk around at night, but I fell down because my legs were weak. But little by little I started to work in the house while nobody was around.

That fall we have to go to Kaiyuh. When they first put me in the boat, they have to cut branches to put on the ground for me to walk. And when we got to Kaiyuh, they wouldn't let me go for berries either. Because, they say, when we pick berries while we're that way we get spotted on our face and brown stripes.

In the boat I had an overparky on and a shawl over it. I sit down and I look down. I could look at things like willows, but not at people. They don't let people look at our face too much because it would spoil our complexion. And we never eat fresh animals. Meat has got to be a week old. I never ate boiled things either. I didn't break any backbones because then my back would be weak and I would get hurt right away. I never had trouble with my backbone.

I wasn't supposed to eat warm things for a year. I didn't stay that way a year because some boys wanted to marry me. This was in July of 1910. The next April I got married. It was a forced marriage. I didn't sleep with my husband for a couple of months because maybe I was too young. And he'll be unlucky if I sleep with him.

I was the last one that was kept away like that. Me and my friend Olivia. My daddy was pretty strict about me. He wanted me to live long and have

Oregon Province Jesuit Archives

"This is me and my husband Peter Esmailka in Nulato 1913. That's the way we used to sew. Peter is wearing reindeer leggings instead of a snowsuit. No snowmachine suits them days. They used to make leggings that go from the ankles to the knees. And the women wear dresses even when traveling. Sometimes we get cold but we wear fur parkies. The rest of the clothes came from Outside. I know I ordered my coat from Montgomery Wards out of the catalog."

good looks. That's why he kept me like that. This happened after I had been living with the doctor and his wife. Too bad it didn't happen while I was with them, then I wouldn't have been in the corner. But it was good experience.

Curt Madison

Going over photographs for this book in Martha Joe's house in Nulato, November 1982. Josephine Mountain, Martha Joe, and Yvonne Yarber.

Chapter Three: Used to Each Other

Forced Marriage

1911 I got married. It was a forced marriage. In the old days it was like that. The girl's parents pick out a boy who is a good worker, good hunter and makes sled and snowshoes. Then the main thing is if he's trapped. It's hard days that time. So they look for their daughter to have a good home and fresh things to eat.

The boy has to bring over a box for engagement. The box has woman's clothes, sewing things, blankets, and things like that. If the girl's daddy keep it, then they get married.

Right after I became a woman, a trunk came into the house. Daddy put it right out. He said the man was no hunter, drank too much and gambled too much. That man was embarrassed and I know people talked about it. But it was hard those days. Right after that another trunk came in. My dad accepted that one. It was Peter Esmailka.

I was fourteen and a half then. Young, but all the girls got married like that. They want us to get married before we go too far, I guess. I was scared. That's why I didn't sleep with my husband right away. He was that way, too. He didn't care much. He was a nice man and I guess his parents told him to do that. It was the old fashioned way a long time ago. Nowadays it's all different.

Peter was nineteen when we got married and he was already working for the N. C. We got married in the church along with David Madros and Cecelia. Afterwards we had a potlatch with food and dancing and lots of presents. The N. C. gave us a complete kitchen outfit. China dishes and everything.

That was the first time I ever tried to square dance. I fell down. Maybe because I was nervous and maybe because I was too young. I had to wear gloves, too, because it was not one year yet that I became a woman. These two old grandmas told me to wear gloves so I wouldn't touch other boys' hands. And they told me not to look at boys so my complexion would be good. My! Forced marriage! That was a long time ago, that.

We lived with my parents afterwards, but we didn't talk to each other much. Just like we don't see each other. We ignore each other. We don't know how to be with boys those days. Finally later on we started to talk to each other. That way we became acquainted. About a month after that he had to go to work on the boat and I went with my parents to fish camp.

Steamboats

When I woke up to life, I know the N. C. Co. was here. My husband worked for them on the steamer *Reliance* and I worked for them, too. For seven steady summers he worked on that boat. All during that time I kept house for the couple that ran the N. C. Store, Clarence Hyde and his wife. Good strong Catholics.

When the *Reliance* came out from the Koyukuk River, it was carrying gold. They used to bring it upstairs in the N. C. and keep it under the bed. This N. C. agent, Mr. Hyde, told me to mind it. I just lock the upstairs door and tell them, "Hey, it's time for me to go home." I go home. He knows it. And I know when to come back in the morning.

Then they wait for the boat to come up from St. Michael. When that boat comes, they load the gold on and take it down to St. Michael and Outside, I guess, wherever they send it.

The big boats, *Schwatka*, *Sarah*, *Susie*, *Hannah*, and *Louise* had huge whistles. Two pipes, three stories high and a pilot house. You could hear them for miles. My cousin used to tell me stories about when they heard the first steamer.

They were scared. He said they ran in the woods and when the boat stopped they didn't understand anything. There was a woman from Holy Cross and they used to holler for her. They want her to talk for them to find out what these men want. She said they wanted wood to be piled right there. This was a little below Kaltag. They wanted wood for the next ship.

The people did that and the next time the boat came, they picked up the wood and gave them some groceries. As much as they thought the wood amounted to, you know.

The people were living their own way and at first they were scared of the groceries. But after they started to eat it, they liked it. They began to work for it.

Sitting: Peter Esmailka, Gabriel, John Bazook; standing: Martha Joe, Olivia Gabriel, sister to Kokrine Kriska, Rose Kokrine. "This must be after 1912, after he quit steamboating he brought home the bracelet I'm wearing."

During the gold rush days those big boats carried lots of passengers. The rails just used to be black with people. Moving up and down to St. Michael where the boats landed from Outside. I never rode on a steamboat, myself. I don't know why. My husband was working on the *Reliance*. They asked me to go but I was scared of the captain. They said he was quite a womanizer. I know lot of people that rode on the boats. Their relatives pay the fare for them, or their husbands were working on the boat and they pay.

Gee, the wages were cheap those days. Seventy-five dollars a month, two-and-a-half a day. Work so hard all summer for that. Sometimes they get off in Tanana after it got cold and come down with a yukon boat after ice ran in the river.

1917 my husband quit the steamboats. That's when I adopted Eddie. He never stepped on a steamboat again after that. Well, when the railroad came through the steamboats mostly quit anyway. Just the *Nenana* ran after that.

Starting a Family

My husband and I got used to each other. I found out I liked being married. Just like I got loose after I was married. I wanted to dance, go anyplace there was fun with my husband. I didn't go anyplace when I was single. Can't do it. They were pretty strict with me.

I got to like the square dance and waltz. Two-step, kick, hesitation waltz and Virginia reel. Nowadays we don't see any of that kind. Little Johnny Mazook (also called Bazook) used to be good on the accordian and some other people played the violin.

We went to Koyukuk for a dance and Ruby for the races. Gold rush days in Ruby, there were lots of people in 1912 and 1913. We'd stop overnight in villages on the way with people.

Then I adopted Eddie Hildebrande, 1917. My Auntie Anna Brush was his mother and his dad was Bill Burke. Her first husband ran away in Tanana,

"My brother Aloysius, my husband's brother George Esmailka and Jack Screw from Kaltag. He used to be married to my cousin. Gee he had a good home. He used to carry mail, too, from Kaltag to Nulato." Circa 1910.

so she got married to Bill Burke. Then when Eddie came to Nulato to live with me, he took the name Hildebrande. It was supposed to be Esmailka.

Then I raised my brother, too. People wanted to take him, but my husband said not to give him away. That was 1914, four years after we got married and I didn't have any kids of my own. I got my own first child, Mabel, in 1919.

Midwives used to put up a stick for the mother to hang from when she had the baby. Then the midwife was right there to catch the baby. That was the only way they had to help each other. When the doctors came here, they didn't do that anymore. The doctors just put them to bed. It is a struggle for them that way, but it was hard the other way, too.

I was surprised when I found out I was going to have a baby. It was nine years after I got married. I ordered little booties, a layette, and some other things. They came before Mabel was born so I had everything for her already. I understood this because I was with White people. When I went to Catholic mission school, we used to make little clothes for babies. The sisters used to give baby clothes to people that couldn't afford them.

I went as far as fourth grade in the mission school. Spelling, arithmetic, geography, history, and hygiene. That's as far as I went but I didn't go through it all. Hygiene is the one I really understood. So I didn't drink or smoke. Now today I still don't use tobacco. I was going to be the same way about liquor, but my first husband started giving me drinks. And he wasn't a drinker, either.

My daddy was watching me pretty close, even after I got married, even after I raised kids, he didn't want me doing those things. Then one day he found out I was taking drinks. Five years after my husband started giving me drinks, he found out.

"Martha, you start to drink?" he asked me in Indian. I didn't say anything. I was scared of him. Still, even I was married. My husband, too, was scared of him. I don't know how he got the words to say, but he told my daddy, "That's me. I'm giving her drinks. I feed her and I'm taking care of her. I thought to myself why should only me take drinks. That's me that's giving her drinks."

Just like he slapped my father's face. Daddy had nothing to say back to him. Way after that he told me in Indian, "Child, don't over drink yourself if you're going to drink." That's all.

I used to drink lots, but since my husband died in '42, I just kind of slacked on it. My second husband gave me drinks, too, but he died so I quit.

That was a good life I had with my first husband. We used to like to go to camp, work at fish, and go to Eagle Island. In 1913 we went up the Novi River to spring out.

February we left here and we stopped at Koyukuk. At Bishop Mountain they chopped spruce trees down and pushed

Martha Joe Collection

"On the left is Harold Esmailka. He's the big shot now. Next is Mary Lidwin, she's Mary Smith now. My husband Peter Esmailka is wearing a muskrat parky I made. Not even a month it took for me to make that parky. I trapped the skins and as soon as I brought them home, I tanned them. The light color is the belly part and the dark lines are the backs. That's how we used to dress ourselves. No jackets those days just pullover parkies. Last on the right is Rudolph Esmailka, my baby son that got drowned. He had six kids himself, four girls and two boys."

them down the bank. We set up tents right on the ice. From there we stopped at Louden, Dave Lewis' Landing, Melozi, and Ruby. We had two nights in Ruby. Me, my brother-in-law Paul, and my husband.

From Ruby we went out the road thirty miles to Long Creek. There was a gold strike there, too. We went down the street with lots of houses. And we could see men going down in the holes digging for gold.

Out of Long Creek the trail goes over to the Novi. On the way we caught moose. Every family had to have two moose skins, one big one and one small one. When we got to camp, we started to work on those skins. I didn't know how to work at it, but these people we went with showed me. Rose Kokrine and Mrs. Jacob. Rose Kokrine was my husband's cousin and she was nice to us. I tanned this calf and cow skin I had.

After the snow was thawing out, the men started ripping lumber for boats. Every one of us had to have a boat. Seven families. They told me when we go out at the mouth of the Novi River, the people look for dry skins. They see if we got dry moose skins in the boat. So the old women make us tan the skins even if we don't know how. And they told us our husbands had to have new gloves. I made two long pairs, for my husband and brother-in-law. Turns out they just fooled us so we would work hard on the moose skin and learn.

It took about a week to go out to the Yukon. As we were coming closer, we had to dig out the new things. The men put on their gloves and rowed.

We drifted all the way back to Nulato, the current comes down anyway. 1913. That's a long time ago. I never thought I was going to live this long.

For five years my husband and I supported another woman with two kids. She was married to my uncle. He was from downriver where I was born. During the gold rush he was hauling stuff over to the Innoko River for miners. He got acquainted with a woman over there and married her. They had two kids. That poor uncle died of some kind of sickness, and was buried over there.

She came over to the Yukon probably because she had no place to stay over there. He was related to people on the Yukon, but it was hard in those days to take care of her with two kids. I had the two kids I adopted already.

She came in here and told me she had no place to stay. My husband said, "Why don't you keep her? You got too much to do around the house, maybe she'll help you."

We were going out to snares those days, us womens, to get something to eat. Rabbits and all that. I didn't stay in the house all the time, so I agreed with him. I thought the help might be good. Five years she stayed with us and after that she got married again. Malga was her name. Her son is living yet, but her daughter died a long time ago. We used to go down to Eagle Island all together. We had two sleds tied together to move our families around. We were tough those days, us womens.

We women didn't have big guns, but I had a .22 Special. I shot a bear with it once. Three of us were drifting down from where we had our fishnets near Eagle Island. That woman I talked about and another friend of mine. I was big, pregnant at the time.

The men were out hunting on the hills. When the berries get real ripe, they used to go after bears. They're easy to catch for them then. They get the bears while they're in the open eating berries.

We were drifting down from where we had our nets. Pretty long ways. Then we saw it. I was steering and I had my .22 Special. I shot the bear and it went in the grass.

There was a boy in camp with grandma, with us womens that are home. He went back up with those other two women and they found the bear dead in the grass. I had shot it right through the throat. They brought it back and we butchered it up. Only us women and our kids there. I had Mabel and Bertha then. I was carrying Celene.

Another time we went over to Innoko River to trap for the winter with my brother-in-law Walter Nollner. I was pregnant again. Not too long after Christmas I got sick with

"Tom Patsy, he's the one that made the song "Eagle Island Blues". He always used to go down that way to trap around Bear Creek. He was a big husky man. He did anything. He used to walk from his camp up to Nulato. That's over eighty-five miles. One year, I think it was 1939, he came drifting down with the ice. My husband and I were already at out camp on Eagle Island. Nine o'clock at night, ice was running, and we heard a shot. We knew it was him because we were expecting him. We went out to the bank with a rope and a hammer.

'Try to get to the shore!' my husband yelled to him. It was dark but we had flashlights. He caught the rope and pulled himself across on top of the ice. He stayed with us then until after freeze-up. When he went back to his camp on the slough he made that song. I wouldn't say who he made that song after because that woman is still living yet." Circa 1914.

pneumonia. I told him to bring me back over.

"I don't want to die out here," I told my husband.

"You're pretty sick, but you're not dead," he said. He started bringing me over land from Innoko River, over those hills. My brother-in-law sent a boy with us. I was in the sled. Bergman and Harold were in front of me.

It took us five days to get to Kaiyuh. Before we got there I was in labor. Nobody around, in a tent, too, and cold. Well, my husband was my midwife. The baby was born at night, twenty-first of February, nineteen hundred thirty-two.

This baby was born and he was holding me like the way we did to each other. He told me he was crying because he thought I was going to die, too. He didn't know what to do. Well, that's my fault anyway. I just wanted him to take me over. I told him, "I don't care if I die with you on the way." He just did what I told him.

He said to me in Indian, "Honey, try to do your best. Try to do what you can, what you know how to do before."

I was a kind of midwife, too, because I'd been with doctors. I had a flannel and a few things made. I had a rabbit skin blanket for the baby and I lined it. I know how to fix up babies. I cut the cord. Then he told me I should baptize her, too. It was a girl. So I baptized her too, because I know those prayers.

The next day my husband said, "Let's stay here for a day." But I said no. I wanted to get to Kaiyuh that night. It was a long day to Kaiyuh but we just kept on going.

I thought I dressed that baby warm, but it was cold. I put her down inbetween with me. It didn't help. It was too cold. Around one o'clock the sounds stopped. She died.

We got to Kaiyuh and stopped overnight. Nobody there. We took the old trail that goes way down where our camp is. The main trail is over the hills. Nobody there and the only house is where we stopped overnight. February twenty-first. I remember those days. The next day they all came out from the village. They were in from camp for Christmas and stayed that long in town. As the days got longer they moved down. The next day we kept going to the village and stayed with my sister.

"This is in front of my house here in 1949. On the left is my older son Bergman, the violin player. Next is Rudolph Esmailka and then Bertha Esmailka. She became Bertha Demoski. In front of her is Lawana, Lawana Sommer now, my youngest daughter. Last is Mary, Mary Smith now. I think Lawana is having her first communion that day."

Chapter Four: My Life Changed

1942

My life changed alot in 1942. I was kind of upset after my husband Peter died and I didn't know what was going on. He died of TB because he worked so hard. I had kids and no way to support them. No aids those days. My husband told me to send Harold and Mary to Holy Cross and that summer, I did.

The Father came to me and asked, "Are you going to send those kids down, Martha?"

"I got nothing. How will I send them down?" I told him. He just start to laugh.

"You get ready with them and God will take care of it," he told me.

I think maybe he sent them down. I don't know how they went down. He didn't tell me. I was just half off that time.

Mary stayed down there seven years. Only Harold came to visit us and stay for awhile. He was going to stay longer but Brother Feltus wanted him back at Holy Cross to learn to be a mechanic. I didn't want him to go because Celene was pretty close to death that time. It was falltime and Brother Feltus wouldn't let him stay.

"Why do they want him? I want him to be here with us when I die," Celene said. But no he had to go so I just let him go.

Then from Holy Cross he joined the army in 1942. Arthur, Aca we called him, was in the Second World War, too. Two of my boys were in there.

I got married to Frank Joe in 1944. He was raised at Halfway, but his parents moved to Kaltag. His daddy's name was Sleepy Joe. Rudolph was seven and Lawana was two when he married me. He's the one that raised Lucy, Delores, Melvin, and this one Stanford.

"*This is in front of our house one Sunday in the spring after everybody came out from the Kaiyuh. Father Jetté took the photograph. That house is still there but it's getting old. My momma and daddy were living with us then so in 1917 we got another house and moved out. We bought this house and ground from John Antoski for thirty dollars. Later my daddy gave the house in this picture to my brother-in-law Joe Stickman.*"

People identified by Madeline Solomon in 1979. Left to right sitting 1. unidentified; 2. Jimmie Silas; 3. unidentified; 4. Peter Kokrine; 5. James Demoski; 6. unidentified; 7. Big William; 9. and 10. unidentified; 11. Papa Willie; 12. Timothy Number Two; 13. unidentified; 14. Jack Patsy. Standing left to right 1. to 9. unidentified; 10. Martha's husband Peter Esmailka; 11. Malemute; 12. unidentified. Circa 1910.

We still traveled around out to camp, because Frank did what I told him. He was down to Eagle Island once with me, too. That was 1945, the last time I was down there. We moved down to trap in the fall where I used to trap with my first husband. We had cabins two places. I used to like being out.

There's a place we call Dinner Camp, *Nagga Tsuhdeel'eel Dinh*, in Indian. It's the middle of the trail from Kaiyuh to Nulato. Now there's nothing. Everything is all willows now. When there were lots of us we made two fires to cook our dinner. It was open and we could see a long stretch. We all had bells on the tow lines of the dogs so we could hear the sleds coming from a long ways off. It was nice to hear those little bells and the big cow bell on the back of the sled.

When my uncle used to come in from Kaiyuh to Nulato to get some sweet things, we used to be on top of the house, me and my brother Aloysius, to try to hear his bells coming back. Then when it's getting dark we hear them and we're just happy.

He brought oranges, candy, and canned fruit. They wrap oranges in a blanket and keep it on the sled so it wouldn't freeze. Canned fruit and gum were just precious to us.

It's Not Easy Being Old

We used to enjoy going out to camp, eating what we liked. I liked to have a fishnet in, but now I can't do it. I'm helpless now. That was our best time. Traveling was the best for us in those days. Now the young generation doesn't know anything about what I'm saying. They don't know our old ways. I try to tell my grandchildren, but they ignore me. They don't want to listen, so I just think to myself. It's no use to talk. I talk for nothing.

None of them understand our language. That makes it hard for us. I'm the oldest one in town. Even the parents don't know. These young generation's parents don't know how to talk Indian.

When I was young, people didn't imagine modern things. My! If those old people were alive now they'd be scared to death. They'd be scared of TV. They'd say *hutɬanee*, that's some kind of spirit that will go against our life. They'd say that. Even me. I'm surprised to see those things.

The first time I saw TV I just thought of the old people. Even now I think of them. I wonder what they would do. I know they'd be scared. They wouldn't even have it on, I bet.

I'm used to it now. I'm glad to have it. For the condition I'm in, you know, alone and lonesome. I like it now. That's my friend. It keeps company with me. I look at it now that I'm alone. I have nobody with me except my grandson.

I like radio, too. I got one from Anchorage this fall but my daughter took it up to Kaiyuh. Radio is all we had before TV. We're used to it. I like to have it instead of TV because sometimes they play old songs.

I gave my radio to my daughter because they're up Kaiyuh all alone. They tell me it's the best radio they ever had. "How you find out that kind of radio?" they ask me. Well, when I was out there in Anchorage they told me that it's a good radio. It plays London, Japanese, and Chinese. My daughter

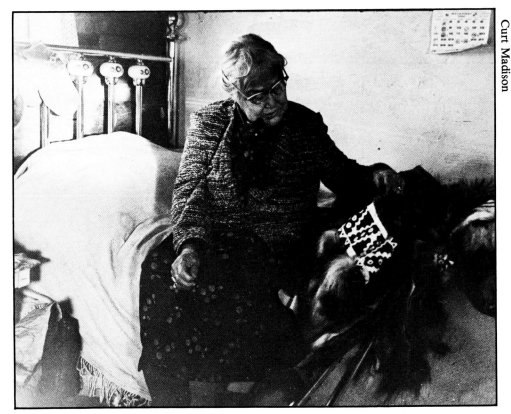

Curt Madison

Martha Joe on her bed examining her most recent fur parky. November 1982.

51

said they hear all those places.

"That's why I bought it," I tell them. She took it out of the cache, you know, and went to Kaiyuh. But I let her have it because she's the only one that is the baby. Gee, they get there fast now.

We used to travel in the wintertime with dog teams and summertime in boats. No inboards in the boat that time, just rowing. And the boys pulling the boat. Nowadays there's nothing to it. We got to Kaiyuh in a couple hours. Round trip in one day. Where it took us three nights to come up sometimes in the summertime.

In the wintertime we used to come up in only one day because of the portage trail like, but we have to start early in the morning. Three o'clock we get up. Start to move around, putting the kids

Nulato Stickdance April 1983. L-R: Julia Nelson, Agnes Jimmy, Martha Joe, Sister Ann Evelyn and Mildred Stickman with their gifts.

in the sled. Finally we start around six. Still it's dark so we got to have a lantern to take us away from camp.

After I was married, even after I had kids, we went out to camp in the fall and spring. We have to be with my parents all the time. The kids went to school, but we take them out. Then when I started to raise my grandson Melvin we stayed in town. Mostly on account of him. After he went to high school, I went out again with my second husband Frank Joe. We used to like to go to Eagle Island. That was the best place because there were not much people to bother like.

My grandchildren don't want to be the way I was raised. Gosh, they want to be only the new way. I wish them to be like the way I was raised, but nobody wants to listen. They just ignore. I want them to learn how to sew and go to fishnet. That's the main thing for us them days. And set snares.

We women didn't keep trapping like the men. We set rabbit snares and whenever we get a chance, if we see tracks, we set traps. That was mostly in Kaiyuh because we just go out from the house.

Nowadays nobody goes out in the fall and spring because we have the government school here. Before we had the sister's school, mission school, and people went out. Since this government school nobody goes. Even some men know how to trap, but they can't go on account of the kids. They're just stuck in town. You see my big grandson here. He's supposed to go out and learn how to hunt and do things. Make something like snowshoes, sled, and fishtrap. He doesn't know anything. I know they're learning something like carpenter stuff, but it's not like the way we used to live.

I can't do nothing no more. I cannot sew. I try to sew or knit but I can't do nothing. I used to make things with all the sewing I did. I was interested to do it them days. I couldn't keep still till I finished. I just want to finish it. Then when I finish it I feel relaxed and happy that I did it. Now I can't do nothing. I'm nearsighted, gee.

I used to see Mamma making things. She used to be a good sewer. She was at Holy Cross. And some girls used to come up from Holy Cross. They stayed with the sisters here. A couple times I used to be with them as I was growing. I see them how they sew. That's how I pick it up, some from here and some from there. That's how I learned.

I did my best not to make mistakes in those days. Nowadays I rip, rip, rip. My! But now I can't do nothing. I've got to have new glasses every year, then I'll do a little sewing. But not fancy sewing. I did a little beadwork this winter for my son Harold's birthday. The kind I used to make for them when they were young. I bet he's just happy. Maybe I'll see him between Christmas and New Year's, spend that time with him.

It's not easy being old. We just take it as it comes. I'm getting weaker and weaker, especially my eyes. It's the worst thing that puts us back. And my legs. I feel like snaring rabbits yet, but I cannot do it. Telling you about it today, the way I did it a long time ago, makes me think about it. I just remember everything. It was so easy those days for us. Nothing to it. I want to do the things I've done again, but I can't.

I really enjoyed snaring rabbits. When we go to the snare and see rabbits hanging down, gee, we feel just happy. I love to go out making snares. Make a fence on the rabbit trail. We set a spring pole and when the rabbit goes in the snare this thing drops down at the end and the rabbit is hanging up.

That's good things to eat, rabbits. That's mostly our food in olden days. Rabbits were mostly our food because there was no moose and no beaver. Nowadays they're all over, moose and beaver. People used to work so hard to catch muskrats in the spring.

Nulato's old community hall. Note the caribou antler on top of the pole. "They make that dance hall in 1912 and put up the pole with caribou antler on top. That's because these people belong to the caribou clan. That's a long time ago and the antler's still up there." April 1983.

Index

Martha Joe's Family Tree

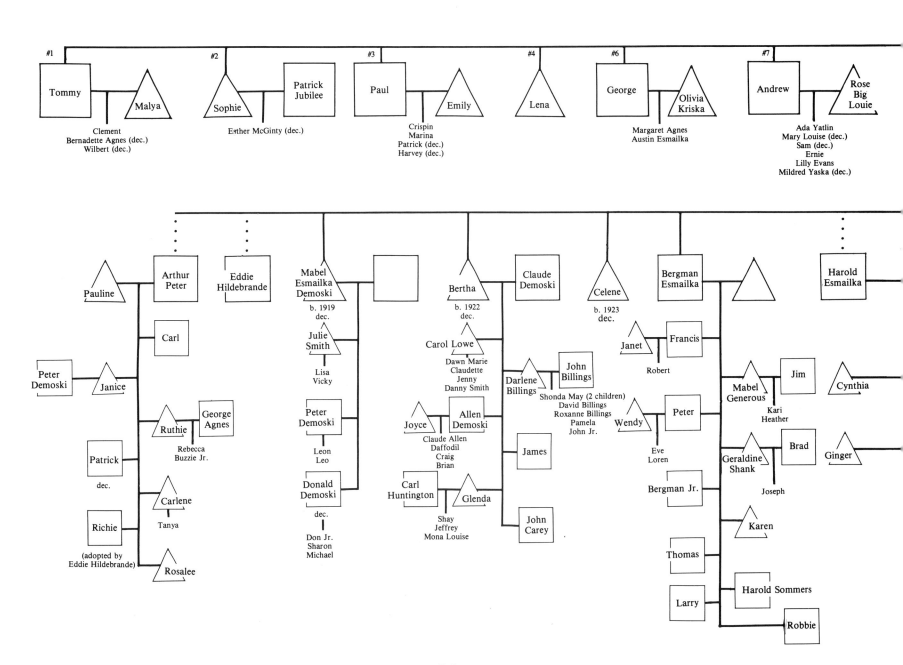

#1 Tommy — Malya
Clement
Bernadette Agnes (dec.)
Wilbert (dec.)

#2 Sophie — Patrick Jubilee
Esther McGinty (dec.)

#3 Paul — Emily
Crispin
Marina
Patrick (dec.)
Harvey (dec.)

#4 Lena

#6 George — Olivia Kriska
Margaret Agnes
Austin Esmailka

#7 Andrew — Rose Big Louie
Ada Yatlin
Mary Louise (dec.)
Sam (dec.)
Ernie
Lilly Evans
Mildred Yaska (dec.)